MW00529154

how's that
working for you?

Make Sure What You Are Doing Produces What You Want!

Cynthia,

#HTWFY

Thank you for
your friend[...]

JASON SCALES

Copyright © 2018 by Jason Scales
All rights reserved. This book or any portion thereof
may not be reproduced or used in any manner
whatsoever without the express written permission of the
publisher except for the use of brief quotations in a book
review.

Limits of Liability and Disclaimer of Warranty

The author and publisher shall not be liable for your misuse
of this material. This book is strictly for informational and
educational purposes. The purpose of this book is to
educate and entertain. The author and/or publisher do not
guarantee that anyone following these techniques,
suggestions, tips, ideas, or strategies will become
successful. The author and/or publisher shall have neither
liability nor responsibility to anyone with respect to any loss
or damage caused, or alleged to be caused, directly or
indirectly by the information contained in this book.

Views expressed in this publication do not necessarily
reflect the views of the publisher.

Cover Design: Studio 5 Agency (www.studio5agency.com)

Printed in the United States of America

ISBN 978-1948270236

Keen Vision Publishing, LLC

www.keen-vision.com

For those who desire to make their dreams a reality.

CONTENTS

INTRODUCTION

The *Voice* is a popular sing-off reality show broadcasted on NBC. On the series, unsigned vocal artists sing their hearts out in hopes that the celebrity judges, who have their backs turned during their audition, will spin their seats around in approval of the chords they passionately belt out. If more than one judge turns around, the contestant then selects which judge will be his or her coach in the following rounds.

One night in 2012, I watched as Bryson Bernard, better known as Cupid, took to the stage and sang a rendition of his song, *Cupid Shuffle*. During his performance, not one of the judges turned around to hit their, "I Want You" button. After he finished singing, the judges turned to face him. They thanked him for his performance and offered feedback. One of the judges, Cee Lo Green, said, "Man, you look familiar!" After realizing he had been busted, Bryson Bernard confessed to being the originator of *Cupid Shuffle*. Cee Lo was astonished. Bryson's hit had made the Guinness's World Record and some of his music had been featured in hit movies. No one understood why the singer decided to audition for *The Voice* after his single *Cupid Shuffle* had been so successful since its release in 2008. When Cee Lo inquired about his reasoning for auditioning, Bryson responded, "I'm on the show because I wanted to be known for being more than the guy who wrote *Cupid Shuffle*."

Cee Lo's next statement encompasses the purpose behind this book. He looked at Bryon and asked, "Then why did you come out here and sing the song you are trying to get away from?" Bryson was dumbfounded. He didn't have a response. After all, how could he? His actions weren't logical. This man represents countless individuals whose behaviors take them in an opposite direction of what they want to accomplish in life. The truth is, many of our actions fail to push us closer to the dreams within our hearts.

If I were a judge on *The Voice* or had an audience of people in this man's predicament, I would ask, "How's that working for you?" This question is more than just the title of this book. It is a phrase I often pose when I preach or counsel. The purpose of this question is not to be condescending or cause a fight. My desire is that this question causes individuals to pause and ask themselves, "Will my current behavior produce what I want to see in my future?" This question allows us to check the effectiveness of our behavior. If we are to ever achieve the things we desire, we must realize when our behaviors are counterproductive. When a behavior does not work, it should be changed.

There are many habits and aspects of our lives that simply do not work; they don't produce the results we want to see in life. Some habits once worked for us, while others never worked in the first place. In order to see results in life, we must decide to put an end to habits and behaviors that don't work.

As a pastor, I have listened to people say, "I can't trust anyone." So, they pull away in isolation, but later complain about being lonely. I ask, "How's that working for you?" I have witnessed spouses who refuse to apologize and own their mistakes and insist that the other person change without stopping to evaluate themselves. Yet, they agonize over having a horrible marriage. I ask, "How's that working for you?" I've seen many situations very similar to these and my question is always the same, "How's that working for you?"

In laymen's terms, insanity is continuously doing the same thing and expecting different results. Here's some good news: The cycle can be broken. One of the greatest signs of maturity is becoming self-aware. One day, while reading the Bible, I made a remarkable discovery that helped me on my journey to self-awareness.

In Romans 7:15, Paul says,

> *"I don't really understand myself, for I want to do what is right, but I don't do it. Instead, I do what I hate."*

Upon reading this very real and raw statement from Paul, I said to myself, "Dang, Paul. You too?" While many would perceive this as a doomsday statement, I saw it as a point of breakthrough. Paul's words indicate that he was aware of his actions, behaviors, and habits. He understood that what he was doing was not working for him. Paul comprehended his need to change even though he was still conforming to old patterns. A problem cannot be changed until it is pinpointed. You must be able to realize that you aren't the problem, however, you have a problem.

This statement by Paul lets us know that it is very possible to do something and hate it. Everyone with bad habits does not necessarily enjoy their bad habits. Many people, like Paul, hate what they partake in, however, can't seem to shake free from the habit. Sounds pretty insane, right? Unfortunately, this is the truth for many of us. Just think about it. How many times have you made a bad decision and beat yourself up about it only to make the same bad decision over and over again? Paul was at this point and honestly, I have found myself in the same predicament in many seasons of my life.

Paul says later in Romans 7:18,

> *"For I know that in me (that is, in my flesh) nothing good dwells; for to will is present with me, but how to perform what is good I do not find."*

Most of us know what to do, we just don't know how or can't find the strength to implement change. Many of us fail to make the necessary adjustments in our behavior because we've not yet made the necessary adjustments in our beliefs. Any and all changes first begin with a change in what we perceive to be true about ourselves and our lives. Within this book, you will:

- Learn practical steps to identify what is not working in your life.
- Discover what does work for you

- Understand how to set in motion the habits and behaviors that will benefit you

This book will serve as a guide to help you identify the blind spots and double standards in your life. As you read, challenge yourself to point out the systems of thinking that hinder your destiny. In the four lessons that follow, I will walk you through the process of becoming more aware of your beliefs, habits, and behaviors. Each lesson consists of real-life scenarios. Together, we will define the problem, determine the solution, and decide how to implement the fix. Finally, we will consider how the principle can be applied to your life. Ready? Let the journey begin.

Identify What's Not Working

Rupert is an extremely bright young man in his early 30s. Rupert is driven, confident in his skills and talents, well-learned, good-looking, and has a good grasp on life. He is well-known for his ability to develop great ideas and problem solve and people always speak highly of his potential.

Rupert is a great dresser, handsome, and makes friends easily. He is also a lot of fun. Everyone enjoys being around him. In his element, he is the life of the party. He causes people to think, laugh, cry, and want to conquer the world in just one conversation. Because of his charisma and intelligence, he never has a problem landing any job he desires. However, once hired, he always runs into the same challenge. When issues on the job become too much for Rupert, he quits and searches for new employment -- until he met Billy Rubin. His encounter with this manager changed his entire life.

Mr. Rubin was more than a manager; he was a phenomenal leader. Rupert immediately loved Mr. Rubin. Mr. Rubin saw Rupert's potential and as a result, afforded him great opportunities. He would allow Rupert to dream by expressing his goals, thoughts, ideas, and aspirations in life. Mr. Rubin's interest in his dreams won Rupert over; he felt like he finally had someone in his corner.

Over time, Mr. Rubin began to observe Rupert's interaction and work relationship with others. He grew concerned about Rupert's behavior. Mr. Rubin noticed that Rupert only performed his best on tasks he thought was important. Additionally, Rupert sometimes completed assignments late, but his work was always so phenomenal that no one dared complain.

After watching Rupert's behavior persist, Mr. Rubin decided to communicate his observations to Rupert. Though Rupert appeared to be understanding and receptive, Mr. Rubin noticed a drastic change in Rupert's attitude after their heart-to-heart. When he would ask Rupert how he was doing, Rupert would sarcastically respond, "I'm swell. Things couldn't be better." Rupert became distant, gave less input, and began to surround himself with groups of coworkers. Mr. Rubin was curious as to what was being discussed in the groups, but he couldn't get Rupert to open up and talk.

Mr. Rubin later found out that Rupert had been using his influence as a gatherer to attract people. In their "meetings," Rupert would point out the issues of the company and how his ideas could make things better if people would listen to him. He began to tell his group that certain things happen when people like him show up. He shared with the group that creatives, such as himself, make stagnant people uncomfortable. Rupert expressed that his great ideas and desire to challenge the status quo made him a target for the disdain of individuals who had grown comfortable and did not want to change.

After he became aware of this unsettling information, Mr. Rubin scheduled a meeting with Rupert to address everything. Rupert was caught off guard and instantly felt offended and attacked. He responded to Mr. Rubin the same way he had responded to previous employers once they'd called him on the carpet about his behavior or actions.

"See! This is what happens to me everywhere I go. I am just going to do my job and keep my ideas to myself," Rupert sighed.

Rupert expected Mr. Rubin to buckle and feel sorry for him. However, Mr. Rubin was an experienced leader, and he'd dealt with individuals like Rupert on several occasions. Instead of playing into Rupert's victim cry, he began to ask Rupert about his previous work experiences. Mr. Rubin had a way of getting people to talk -- even when they didn't want to. He could always pull the best out of people. Rupert began to tell Mr. Rubin about his past experiences, and Mr. Rubin immediately noticed a trend in Rupert's life. He stopped Rupert in the middle of his spill and asked him a question, "Rupert, do you trust me?" This question caught Rupert off guard.

"Well, I guess I don't have a reason not to," he responded.

"Rupert, I have been doing this for a long time," Mr. Rubin said. "You are extremely talented, and you have an incredible future ahead of you. May I share something with you? I believe it will help you accomplish the life goals you shared with me." Rupert's demeanor shifted when Mr. Rubin mentioned his future.

"Sure," Rupert responded with a straight face. He didn't want to appear moved.

"I have noticed how you work and interact with people. Why do you think you run into so many challenges at work?" Mr. Rubin asked.

"Most people aren't that smart," Rupert responded. "They don't think as I do, and they can't handle my confidence."

"So, let me get this straight – your genius is a blessing and a curse? Your expansive knowledge has created some bad situations for you because people can't handle it?" Mr. Rubin asked for clarity.

Rupert nodded his head and smiled, "Yes, sir. Finally! Someone who gets me."

Mr. Rubin looked him square in the eyes and asked, "How's that working for you?" Rupert, caught off guard again, sat there speechless. In his mind, he knew that his current train of thought and behaviors weren't working for him. He was internally frustrated because things were not flowing the way they should. "Rupert, I used to be the same way! I had all the answers, but I kept running into problems. One day, it hit me, and I had to ask myself, 'What good is it to have the answer if no one will ask you a question?' I finally had to admit that I was not building good relationships. I wouldn't listen, I was never wrong, and I was not a team player. I did great work, but it was always on my timetable. I didn't think of how my behavior impacted others. I was a classic deflector," Mr. Rubin explained.

"What is a deflector?" Rupert asked.

"A deflector is someone who doesn't recognize their problems," Mr. Rubin explained. "They can point out flaws in everyone and everything around them but are completely oblivious to the problems within themselves. While the flaws they see in their surroundings may be legit issues, the real problem is that they can't point out the flaws in their actions and behaviors. At some point, they have to realize that pointing out others' problems won't solve their problems."

"So, you're saying I'm a deflector?" Rupert asked.

"I'm saying that you and I have a lot in common, Rupert. I have always been a gatherer -- just like you. I had a way of building a following so that I could discount the truth I needed to hear. I had a habit of discrediting truth bearers. I had to realize that my following consisted of fans and not friends. I had to learn how to use my gifts to build something that benefits the world. I have another question for you, Rupert. Before you answer, I want you to take a second and think about it. Okay?" Mr. Rubin requested.

"Okay," Rupert agreed.

"You've been doing a lot of deflecting lately. How's that working for you?" Mr. Rubin asked softly.

Rupert sat for a moment and thought to himself. He already knew the answer to Mr. Rubin's question. It wasn't working for him. Even though he was right in many situations, he was not winning. He admitted to Mr. Rubin that he needed to change some things in his life, and the two began to create systems to help Rupert become the individual he had the potential to be.

Jason Scales

LET'S TALK ABOUT IT

If we were in Mr. Rubin's shoes, many of us would have probably been just a tad bit frustrated. After all, Rupert's issue was clear from the beginning. You were probably able to pinpoint early on that Rupert had an issue within himself that caused him to jump from job to job. I'm sure it was fairly easy for you to highlight the issue with Rupert well before his chat with Mr. Rubin. The truth of the matter is, it is always effortless for us to pinpoint what is not working for others. However, when we are in front of the mirror, it's not always as easy to see the 4x4 slab of plywood hanging from our eyelid.

Unfortunately, many of us don't realize that our behaviors are working against us until we experience failure. Like Rupert, we are given several opportunities to learn from our behaviors, however, we choose to magnify the environmental issues while completely ignoring our internal issues. We all decide how and when we will learn. We are always given the choice of whether we will learn from the School of Hard Knocks or the Academy of Wisdom. They both present learning opportunities daily, however, many of us ignore the quiet promptings of wisdom until we are knocked down and forced to listen.

One would think that pinpointing our unfruitful behaviors is an easy task. After all, anyone with common sense should be able to view their lives, realize what isn't working, and quickly adjust their behavior, right? Wrong. This is actually one of the hardest things to do. Some behaviors are so deeply ingrained within us that we can't see our reality past our dysfunction.

Issues vs Injuries

The first step to pinpointing dysfunctional behaviors is to identify your issues. We often mistake injuries for issues. Our injuries are circumstances that damaged us. Issues are the shortcomings or flaws we are born with or the lingering impact from prior injuries in our lives. Issues you are born with may be generational or something you have dealt with from birth. Since I was a child, I've struggled with being neat. Nothing happened to cause this issue, it's just something I've always struggled with. On the other hand, issues that are lingering impacts from prior injuries could be the fact that you were embarrassed at an early age by an authority figure and now, as an adult, any perceived aggressive action from an adult triggers that experience. Our issues, when impacted by our current injuries, have the potential to shape our approach in life. Our injuries cause us not to see things as they are, but rather as we are.

Personally, I struggled with fear and becoming overwhelmed by pressure for most of my life. When I began to play sports, these issues really began to affect me. In high-pressure games against great opponents, I would get extremely nervous and not perform at my peak ability. I turned into a completely different player. However, when there was no pressure, I was one of the greatest athletes on the field.

During a baseball game when I was ten years old, I got hit by the ball. I was in the batter's box, ready to swing and take off. When the pitcher threw the ball, it hit my ankle.

The pain was excruciating. One of my bones cracked, my leg was bruised badly, and I had a blood clot. It was a horrible experience, but it eventually healed.

That same year, I made the All-Star team. All-Stars were the top performing athletes from our league who competed against the top athletes from other cities' leagues. During All-Star practice, I faced the same pitcher who had hit me in the ankle earlier in the season. I couldn't stay in the batter's box for fear that I would be hit again. My coach got angry and cursed at me. His "motivation" encouraged me to face my fear. I stood in that box and started hitting the ball with a vengeance. If I knew then what I know now I would have asked myself, "Jason, how is that working for you?"

Running from the ball and being scared did not work. It took a lot to overcome my fear, but I did it. Though it appears that my fear was caused by the injury, that was not the case. The injury only exposed the greater issues within me. The root of my problem was my fear and inability to deal with pressure. Was being hit by the ball painful? Yes! Was my ankle actually hurt? Yes! However, in the game of baseball, people get hit pretty often while batting. Most people bounce back fast and never think any more about the hit. My bounce back took longer because of the issues that already existed within me.

If you are ever going to make any changes in your life, you must first separate your issues from your injuries. Nothing will get fixed if you focus on the wrong thing. While it is necessary to heal from your injury, don't forget to deal with the underlying issues. Focusing on the injury alone causes you to play the victim and become defensive and very guarded. When you focus on your injury and role as a victim, you pass up the opportunity to become your true self. Dealing with your issues is not about placing the blame on others. It requires you to take responsibility for your behavior. While a victim asks, "Why do they always talk about me?" someone who desires to deal with their issues asks, "Why does it bother me so much when people talk about me?" See the difference?

While it is easy to blame others for your current state, that doesn't change anything. Yes, some people aren't untrustworthy. Yes, things have happened to you that were unfair. But, you can move on and be better. Injuries may be bad, but your previous issues make them worse than what they should be. We must stop treating the symptoms and take the steps necessary to get to the root of our problems. Investigate why certain things have such a great impact on you. When you identify your issues and began to work on them, you will move forward in life.

TASK ONE

Take a moment to identify your issues and the injuries that caused you to see them. Be sure to separate your issues from your injuries!

You Don't Know What You Don't Know

One of my dear friends participated in a race. The night after the race, her family called to inform us that she had been admitted to the hospital. We were shocked and wondered if something had gone wrong during the race. When my family arrived at the hospital, we learned that she'd had a heat stroke during the race. I was completely caught off guard. Months before the race, she had trained extensively; so, I knew she was prepared for the race. I didn't understand what had gone wrong.

"What did it feel like when you had the stroke?" I asked.

"At first, I felt myself getting faint," she explained. "I told myself, 'You are not going to quit. You are going to push thru this! The next thing I know, I woke up in the hospital."

The doctor said that even though she was in good shape for the race, her body was not hydrated enough to run a race in that type of heat. Her body couldn't perspire and bring her temperature down fast enough, so she overheated. It's a blessing that she is still here with us.

Her situation made me realize something very vital to our success. It doesn't matter how determined we are to accomplish something; if we aren't prepared, we will not see the results we desire. Unfortunately, ignorance is not bliss. Ignorance keeps us clueless about the behaviors and habits that are not working for us. Yes, many times, we are doing all we know to do. But, at some point, we must step back and assess if we know everything we need to know to accomplish our goals.

Ignorance can derive from immature areas in our lives. When we are immature, we can be overzealous due to a lack of exposure and experience. In many situations like these, everyone can see our immaturity -- but us. I cringe when I think of some of the things I have said and done out of ignorance. I have made decisions before acquiring all the facts needed. I have made ineffective declarations out of passion instead of wisdom. I have missed many opportunities because I was completely ignorant of the potential they were loaded with. For quite some time, I was oblivious that there was a world outside of my experience and exposure.

I am not good at golf, but I like playing. One day, a buddy of mine took me to the driving range to give me a golf lesson. While we were there, I noticed a father and his teenage son arguing. I thought to myself, "Great. Another father who is living out his athletic dreams through his son who probably doesn't even like golf." However, once I got closer, I realized the story was completely different. I approached the father and inquired about his son's age and progression in golf. As if he had been waiting for someone to vent to, the father let it rip. "Do you know what is wrong with my son?" he asked.

With dread, I responded, "What?"

"Success," he said. "My son hit a hole in one at the age of 12, and now he is 15. He is in a slump, and he is not progressing. He can't seem to figure out why. He blames his stagnation on me and everyone else. He doesn't realize that he is not maximizing his potential. Since that hole in one three years ago, he has been trying to prove to the world how good he is. He refuses to allow people to help him become better. He is stuck in the place of his last success."

This struck me like a bolt of lightning. Before this instance, I never thought that success could keep us from growing. Success should be the catalyst to discover our potential. However, for many, it provides a place for pride to set in. Pride says to us, "You have tasted success at this level of operation. There's no need to improve." Pride causes us to become complacent at our current level of productivity. We remain ignorant of how much better we could become if we sought wisdom. Pride limits our ability to grow. This is detrimental because as long as we are living and breathing, we should be growing in every area of our lives. What worked for us five years ago may not be working now. However, we will never realize this if we allow pride, ignorance, and immaturity to hold us to where we currently are. At every point of success or failure, we need to seek wisdom on how we can improve.

TASK TWO

Find three people you trust to be honest with you and ask them the following questions:

- What's holding me back in life?
- What are people not telling me about myself?
- What do I need to change to be a better _____?

Double Standards

Sometimes we have higher expectations for others than we have for ourselves. We expect others to dot every 'i' and cross every 't,' however, we allow ourselves more space to make mistakes. We are an attorney for our shortcomings, but a judge for the failures of others. We judge others by their actions and ignore their intentions, but judge ourselves by our intentions and disregard the inconveniences our actions may cause. For instance, I hate to be cut off when I speak, but I do it to people all the time.

I know individuals who value being able to express creativity and work outside of the box, however, when they are in authority, they force everyone to abide by their rules and standards. Most of us are completely unaware of our double standards until we are confronted with the truth of our ways.

As we previously discussed, Paul expresses his frustration with living by double standards in Romans 7:15. His statement, "The very thing I hate, that I do," is a direct example of living by double standards. We detest certain behaviors and habits in others, but fail to realize that we do them ourselves. You despise when others are inconsistent, however, your follow-through sucks. Maybe you dislike ineffective communication, but you don't know how to properly express your feelings without yelling. Or, you don't like junky or cluttered environments, however, your home is never cleaned or organized. The list goes on and on.

The truth is, much of the frustration we have with our environment derives from the disappointment we have with ourselves that we have not dealt with. Instead of directing it inward, we tend to lash out at everything around us, like our friend Rupert. As we discussed before, it is very easy to point out the flaws around us. After all, we're not on the receiving end of the critique we are issuing. It's easier to pressure others to change than it is to realize that we have to make some changes within ourselves.

The first step to recognizing our double standards is refocusing our attention and judgment. We must put less effort into pointing out the issues around us and put that energy into pinpointing the issues within us. True maturity is marked by our ability to critique our lives, in the same manner, we are inclined to critique others.

When we live by double standards, we put the pressure for change on everything but ourselves. We wait for others to change or shift before we make the necessary moves in our lives. The sad reality is that when you put yourself in this position, you may never change. People, in this situation, only change after realizing within that it is time to make a change. If you never see a need to change, you will become stuck with your frustrations with others and never recognize the changes you need to make within yourself.

Blind Spots

Honestly, we don't see as much of the world as we think. We need the truth in love and people to help us in those areas. For some of us, our blind spots are things people won't tell, have told us, or common themes that keep occurring in our lives that have gone unattended. When we have these types of blind spots, life is just a train wreck waiting to happen. Very often, when people try to advise us or warn us, we write them off as haters. We feel as though anything that conflicts or contradicts what we think or desire are attacks from hell designed to make us quit. This isn't always true, but when this is our perspective, we never experience the growth we need to achieve our goals. If you are not going in the direction of your goals, you won't reach them. It's like desiring a certain restaurant but going in the opposite direction of the GPS. At some point, you must stop and ask yourself, "Are my actions taking me closer to my goals or leading me further away?"

After my wife and I were married, I began to gain weight. One day, I was moving something, and my wife looked at me and asked, "Why are you sweating and breathing so hard?"

Taken aback I said, "What are you talking about? No, I'm not."

She gently took me by the hand and led me to a mirror. "Look," she said.

I cautiously looked at myself in the mirror. Lo and behold, I was sweating and breathing hard. I had no clue. Growing up, I was extremely skinny, so that is how I viewed myself -- even into my adulthood. I still saw myself as a skinny kid and was unaware of my reality.

We have blind spots because we perceive that we are known for our potential -- not our reality. We shut ourselves off from the rest of the changing world. Just because you don't believe something doesn't mean it's not true. When many of us discover we have blind spots, our reactions are varied. Our most common response is denials. We say things like:

"I don't have a problem."
"If I was that bad, I wouldn't be as successful as I am!"
"Nobody else has ever said that about me."
"Well, everyone else is okay with the way I operate, they just need to get with the program."

The biggest issue is that we are more offended by others pinpointing our blind spot than the actual blind spot itself. Crazy, right? When our blind spots are highlighted, we've been so oblivious to them that our pride causes us to discredit the source that spotted them. We are often not ready to hear what we didn't know. Then, immaturity steps in and causes us to become secretly self-conscious about every other area of our lives. We over-correct, get paranoid, and operate in shell shock. We walk on eggshells so to speak. These are the incorrect responses to revealed blind spots. Understand that you will always have blind spots; they create our need for God and relationships. However, you can live beyond your blind spots once you recognize them and start to address them. Here are a few ways you can ensure that you live beyond your blind spots:

Live as broken in success as you do after failure.

When we fail, especially openly, we are usually determined to do something different and make changes in our lives. However, if we are not careful, success can cause us to become smug and complacent. In the same way that you analyze your actions after failure, examine them after success. Evaluate what you did, what went well, and what could have been better. Open yourself to critique after every victory just as you would after failure. Be open to hearing, "Yeah, that was good, but you could have done this better."

Develop healthy relationships.

Again, blind spots are unavoidable. I don't care how much an automobile maker advertises that their newest models have no blind spots, there are always blind spots. Typically, you never realize them until you have or almost have a car accident. In the same way, we will always have blind spots. Just as an attentive passenger can shout, "Hey!

Watch that car over there!" the right people in your life can do the same thing. Find people who love you and will speak truth to you. Trust individuals who speak your language and can help you see both sides of the story. Ask God to staff your life with more friends and fewer fans. Fans will tell you all the good about you and make light of your need to improve. Friends will see the great, but they won't be afraid to tell you where you need to improve. They will provide you with the insight you need to improve and become the person God has created you to be...the person you ultimately desire to become.

Submit to authority.

We all need authority in our lives. Our lives require the voice and presence of those who make us tighten up, shut up, and listen when they come around. Submit to authoritative individuals who speak your language. Allow them to provoke and push you to the next level.

Repent and embrace the truth.

Staffing your life with friends and those you respect is pointless if you don't embrace the truth they give you. Once truth is spoken, you must embrace it. This requires maturity; receiving truth forces us to grow up. Maturity can be measured by the amount of time it takes you to respond to truth. When you hear the truth about yourself, instead of running away, your response should be to repent and seek God about how you can make the necessary adjustments in your life. Truth is from God and is spoken by those in our lives through the Holy Spirit. When we understand this, we can look past the earth suits of the individuals who reveal our blind spots and appreciate their honesty.

Realize that there's life beyond blind spots.

Often, our greatest discoveries happen after we realize our blind spots. Humility happens and the doors open for learning and growth in our lives. Understand that failure caused by blind spots are not the end of the world. I love reading about King David. In the Bible, we see that David experienced many failures due to his blind spots. After his debacle with Bathsheba and her husband, the prophet Nathan confronted David about his blind spot. David responded with humility and repentance. After his restoration, the Bible records the following in 2 Samuel 12:14,

> *"And David comforted Bathsheba, his wife, and went in unto her, and lay with her: and she bare a son, and he called his name Solomon: and the Lord loved him."*

Isn't it amazing that the wisest man said to have lived was birthed after David's greatest mistake? Identifying what is not working in your life requires that you address your issues, ignorance, double standards, and blind spots. If you are not afraid to confront your blind spots head on, you too will give birth to some of your most amazing victories and open your world up to success you never imagined.

Identify What's Working

S ilas is a charismatic young man with big dreams. He is well connected and has friends from every culture, background, age, and ethnicity. One of his biggest dreams is to establish a business. After graduating from high school, Silas set off to college to major in entrepreneurship with a minor in finance. Unfortunately, Silas was not mentally prepared for college. Even though his mind was set on what he wanted to accomplish, he lacked discipline. Additionally, his new freedom allowed him to make bad decisions. His inquisitive nature, need for adventure, and love for people caused him to get involved with the wrong crowds and experiment with illegal activity. Silas knew that his illegal habits could cost him his future, but he just couldn't seem to shake them. The peer pressure from the individuals he hung out with made him believe his actions were okay.

For his first summer break, Silas went home with his parents and brought his illegal habits right along with him. His parents picked up on his new habits immediately, but, they didn't think it was too serious. Silas was a good kid, so they sat him down, talked with him about his decisions, and assumed their troubles were over. One day, Silas ran into issues with the authorities, and his parents had to sacrifice a lot to get him out of trouble. They were irate and heartbroken. They couldn't believe that their son was so deeply intertwined with illegal activities. They decided to talk to him, but this time, their conversation wasn't as light.

"Silas, what you are doing is downright pathetic. You made all of these ambitious goals for yourself. Where on earth do you think your current habits will take you?" Silas' mother asked.

"It's simple," his dad responded. "If you continue on this path, you will destroy your future and never own any business. You would be lucky to clean the floors at a business." His mother nodded silently in agreement.

His dad's statement infuriated him, "Don't you dare speak that over my life. I am going to be successful, and I will have several businesses!" Silas shouted.

"We don't have to speak that over your life, Silas. Your decisions and attitude are speaking that over your life," his father replied. This statement stopped him in his tracks. His parents had never spoken to him this way. As a matter of fact, no one ever spoke to him this way. Silas finally heard the truth about himself. He knew they were right.

Once his parents realized they had his attention, his dad asked, "If you continue on the path you're on, where do you think you will end up?"

Silas couldn't answer. He knew the road he was on was destined for destruction. His mom looked at him and said, "How are your current habits and behaviors working for you?"

He put his head down and mumbled, "They aren't working."

"Silas, our decisions are like the money we deposit into an account," his mother explained. "We have to ask ourselves if our actions are funding our dreams or our downfalls."

That night, Silas decided that he needed to change. He knew he had to decide between saving up for his dream or funding his downfall. He did some soul searching and realized that he was not living up to his potential. He knew that his actions would not push him to become all he desired to be. After that night, Silas made some decisions to change the course of his life.

TASK THREE

Before you read another word ask yourself, "If I continue on my current path, where will I end up?" Then, ask someone who loves you and knows your life goals to answer this question for you as well.

Jason Scales

LET'S TALK ABOUT IT

We may not be into illegal activities like Silas, but many of us share his mindset: We speak success but live failure. We often decree and declare things over our lives that we don't take action to make happen. This phenomenon creates a life cycle we don't realize we are living in. Cycles are often hard to identify in our own lives but easy to identify in the lives of others. The reason they are hard to identify in our own lives is because we can have an objective view of others' lives and an emotional view of our own. Emotions can often cloud our vision and cause us to see things as we are instead of how they are.

When we view our mishaps, we think of everything that happened around the time of our failure. We say things like:

"I made a bad decision because I was tired."
"I was dealing with a lot of grief at the time."
Or,
"I was dealing with so much spiritual warfare."

When we view the mistakes others, on the other hand, we say things like:

"They should have known better."
"They have been doing this for years."
Or,
"They need to pray, fast, and seek God more."

We take away the fact that they may have been tired, grieving, or fighting, and only see what they should have

31

done differently. This lets us know that we have the capability to see what does not work. However, in order for us to make any changes in our lives, we have to turn that trained, objective eye toward our own life cycles. We must view every aspect of our lives practically and objectively if we desire to reach our goals. Let's dive into steps for pinpointing what will work for our lives.

Step 1: Figure Out What You Want

If you don't know what you desire, it is impossible to achieve anything. After all, how can you appropriately track your progress if you don't know what you're working towards? I know you may be thinking, "Well, duh!" but this step is not as common as you may think. Many of us have an idea of what we want, but we don't have all the details. Most of the time, the excitement of having a desire or vision causes us to miss the most important step: Sitting down to pinpoint what it actually looks like. We say things like, "I want to be a good spouse," or "I want to run a successful business." However, we fail to pinpoint what success in these areas looks like to us. As a result, we find ourselves in a rat race, trying to obtain what the world says success looks like. When we come up short, we are aggravated or frustrated. In this state, it is unlikely that our actions or behaviors are productive. Again, if you don't know what you are working towards, you have no idea what to work or how to work it!

Discover what you want by identifying what is in your heart in this season. All of your passion, revelations, and ideas flow from what is in your heart. What is driving you in this season? Now, this isn't for you to drop your responsibilities, quit your job, and go live some lifelong dream. Think more about what you wish to accomplish where you already are. How can you improve the condition of your life with the opportunities that have already been afforded to you? Take a moment and think about all of your current responsibilities and your roles. What do you want to come from them? It could be a desire to go back to school, lose weight, get out of debt, land a better job, be a better spouse or parent, etc. Pinpoint where you are and what you ultimately desire.

TASK FIVE

Write down what you want. On another sheet of paper, write down what you are doing to get there.

Step 2: Set Your Course In That Direction

Once you determine what you want, you must begin to walk towards it. As humans, we are creatures of habit. It is difficult to convince ourselves that certain behaviors or habits aren't working for us. We can be great people, treat everyone right, and have great motives, but that alone doesn't guarantee success in life. To accomplish our goals, we must ask ourselves the tough questions. Start with this question: What actions, habits, or behaviors aren't working or producing what you want? You must pinpoint what never worked or no longer works and redirect your path. One indicator of self-awareness is when you can identify when a habit or method has run its course. Methods have an expiration date, but your ability to produce and your destiny in life will never expire.

This step requires a level of honesty that may be painful. However, it's necessary if you ever desire to become the person you want to be. Take a look at your lists from Task 5 and evaluate what you are doing to meet your goals. From the looks of things, are you on track to get where you desire to be? For example, it could be in your heart to lose weight. When most people have weight-loss goals, the first thing they do is buy a treadmill and a gym membership. However, the most effective place to start is evaluating your current activity and diet. Do you have behaviors, actions, or habits that will slow the progress of your weight loss? Allow me to introduce you to Mark.

Mark wakes up at 7:00 am to arrive at work by 8:00 a.m. He grabs the breakfast special at a local restaurant: Two sausage egg and cheese biscuits with a Pepsi. Mark goes to work and works hard until it's time for lunch. He doesn't have a lot of time for lunch, and he's on a budget, so he grabs his favorite from the closest fast food restaurant: Two double cheeseburgers, a small fry, and another Pepsi. He gulps his food down in the car, rushes back to work, and goes non-stop until 5:30 pm. After work, he rushes to pick up his kid from school and take him to practice. Once practice is over at 7:00 pm, he and his kid meet the wife at a local pizza buffet. Once he gets home, he is super tired. He helps his kid with

Jason Scales

homework, talks to his wife, and goes straight to bed. This is his daily routine.

Are there any similarities in your life and Mark's daily routine? I sure hope not. A life set up like this will not help anyone lose weight. They would need to make some serious changes to their schedule and eating habits. If not, they will become frustrated and continue to waste money on workout equipment and gym memberships. In scenarios like these, even things that should work won't work if they aren't used properly. Unhealthy eating and lifestyle habits will cancel out a great run at the gym any day. With this type of routine, they will eventually fall into fast weight loss schemes, cancel the gym membership, sell the treadmill, and, in frustration, punish things that do work.

Treadmills and gym memberships help people lose weight all the time, but it won't work for an individual with a routine similar to Mark's routine. Just as with other goals, the other pieces of weight loss like eating right and being active work together with working out. If you were Mark, what changes would you make to your schedule to achieve your weight loss goals? As you look at your goals and activity, evaluate them with the same objectiveness. Thinking objectively and asking the tough questions will get you to the root of what is not working in your life.

TASK SIX

Objectively evaluate your goals and current activity.

35

Another way to determine if things aren't working is to gauge the pressure in your life. Sometimes, life will tell you when things are not working. Thank God for weird moments and feelings. They force you to look at yourself and your methods in life. Pressure is not a bad thing at all. Sometimes, we perceive life pressure the wrong way. There will be seasons where we may have demands and complaints from every side. We could even feel like nothing we do is right or good enough. Instead of shutting down, fussing, or retaliating, take a look at yourself. Is it time to mature or shift gears? Have you lost your momentum? Do you need to make some changes to light your fire again? Seasons of pressure are our greatest opportunity to make tremendous shifts! Pressure is not the end of the world. Yes, I know it may feel like everything is falling apart, but seize the moment to make everything come together. There is always another level in you. Where do you need to shift gears and operate at the level of the demand in your life?

Step 3: What Do You Need to Produce What You Want?

Now that you know what is in your heart and have determined what is not producing what you desire, you should be able to identify what you need to create what is in your heart. This step requires you to research, find a mentor, and study how to carry out what is in your heart. This step will not only awaken something inside of you to dream, work, and live beyond where you are, but it also impacts your decision making. You will begin to add and delete things in your life based on your desired direction. In this step, you will begin to experience freedom because you will learn what to say no to and what to say yes to. You will know what works by asking the simple question, "Is this going to produce what is in my heart?"

TASK SEVEN

In your tablet or journal, answer these questions.

What or who do you need to add to your life to produce what is in your heart? What do you need to take away from your current routine or schedule?

LESSON THREE

Learn How To Work What Works

At the age of seven, Hazel knew she was different. It wasn't because of her long kinky hair or her oversized glasses; she was extremely gifted and talented. She was born and raised in what most would consider "the hood." Quite naturally, she was sometimes teased and bullied because she was smarter than most of her peers. Hazel's neighborhood didn't exactly take pride in education. In fact, people were just happy that their sons graduated before getting locked up and that their daughters made it to high school before getting pregnant. Hazel was accustomed to hearing gunshots before breakfast, walking around homeless people passed out in the middle of the sidewalk, and staying close to her mother or father when they were riding the bus.

Though her environment at times seemed hopeless, Hazel's parents kept a strict system in their home. They made sure that Hazel studied, did her homework, and read every night. Though they only had a high school diploma themselves, they were determined to see more for their little girl. When Hazel turned thirteen, her mother and father got additional jobs so that they could send her to a better school. They knew their daughter was different, and they wanted to make sure she got the same academic advantage as other children.

Hazel's school was on the other side of town, about 23 miles away from her home in the projects. Hazel and her mother had to catch three buses to get there every morning. They were never late. Even when it rained or snowed, Hazel was always at her desk before the homeroom bell rang. The day Hazel walked across the stage at graduation made it all worth it. Hazel acquired a scholarship to attend one of the best schools in the country. After graduating magna cum laude, she landed a job at one of the top finance firms in her home state.

Three years later, Hazel sits across from her boss fighting to maintain her composure after receiving the worst review in her life. Her boss felt that she was not a team player and that Hazel did not stick to the company's way of getting things done. Her boss made it very clear that if these things did not change, Hazel would have to find a new place of employment.

As she sat in the chair across from her boss, she tried her best to remain calm. On the inside, however, she was afraid of losing her job, embarrassed of her inadequacies, and hurt by the severity and harshness of her boss's review. A thousand thoughts ran through her mind. Her first reaction to her boss was to discount his review. She was the only African American on the team, and her boss was a Caucasian male. Maybe he can't take my assertiveness, she thought to herself. Hazel had always stood out and marched to the beat of her own drum. Hazel had often felt awkward in team meetings and company outings. As a result of feeling this way, she became defensive. Suddenly, Hazel could keep it in no longer. As tears rolled down her face, she let out everything that was going through her mind.

"With all due respect, Mr. Ashton, your review is not fair. I am here at work on time every day. I even stay late to get things done. I take my lunch in the office. I don't gossip. I even pull the weight of other people. I don't think that it's fair that you are coming down so hard on me when there are people in this building who don't work half as hard as I do. I don't work well with them because all they do is talk and laugh all day. I am here to work...not make friends, Mr. Ashton," she ranted.

Mr. Ashton was not moved. He finally stopped her and said, "Hazel, I don't disagree with what you have said, but my main comment remains. You need to be more of a team player, and you need to work the system that we have in place here. You appear to be really upset right now. Please take the rest of the day off to think about what I've said."

Hazel gathered her things and left quickly. As soon as she got out of the door and into her car, she called her best friend, Byron. Byron worked in finance as well. They had been best friends since high school. Byron was extremely intelligent and was a no-nonsense type of guy. Hazel often joked that everyone needed a Byron in their lives. He was trustworthy and had a great way with words. He was one of the few people Hazel would stop and listen to without many rebuttals.

"Byron! I can't believe what Ashton just said to me. I work my butt off for this company, and he had the nerve to tell me that I'm not a team player and that I don't adhere to the company's systems. Then, he dismissed me like I was some mad black woman! Ugh!" Hazel ranted.

"Well, is he right?" Byron asked calmly.

"What? About me being a mad black woman?" Hazel snapped.

Byron laughed. "Well, yeah. That too. But mostly the other part. Are you a team player? Do you overlook the company's systems?"

Hazel was stunned. "Byron, you just don't understand. I'm the only black person on his team. I feel like he is just giving me a hard time because he accepted my resume before he saw this skin and hair of mine. After all, how many black girls from West Philly have a name as simple as Hazel. He's just mad because I'm smarter than the rest of those Susans, Billys, and Catherines he hired! I worked hard to get where I am! My mother and I traveled 23 miles every morning from....."

"Hazel, listen to me." Byron began. "You're being extremely stubborn right now. Your defense is all the way up, and you are not listening to your boss. How is that working for you?"

Hazel rolled her eyes. She knew Byron was right. "Okay, though the race thing may be an issue, I know it's not the issue here."

"Think about this, and you don't have to answer me right now. What do you really want to say to your boss?" Byron asked.

Deep in her heart, she knew what she wanted to say to her boss. She wanted to tell him that he was correct and ask for his advice. However, that is not what she did. Once she made it home, Hazel sent an email requesting another meeting with her boss the next day. Hazel didn't want to ask for his assistance. She felt that being a team player and following the company's system was something everyone else already knew, so she would just have to figure it out on her own. In her mind, she just needed to get back in good standing with her boss long enough to show him that she could be better.

The next morning, Hazel stopped by the nearest doughnut shop and brought the team doughnuts and a smile before she went into her meeting with her boss. When it was time for the meeting, she looked her boss in the face and said, "By this time next year, things will be different. I will have an E-ranking, and we will never have this conversation again."

"So, what are you going to do differently?" her boss asked without looking up at her. This stunned Hazel. She had no answer. She wanted to do better, she knew she had the potential to do better, but she didn't know where to begin. She knew she needed to humble herself, tell him that she didn't know, and ask for help. She just couldn't bring herself to do it. Though she was in over her head, she refused to come across as incompetent. So, she sat there in silence.

"Listen, Hazel. You have a lot of potential. You are smart, and you can do the job. You haven't accepted the fact that being smart is not good enough." Mr. Ashton explained.

Hazel looked up at her boss. She was so confused. For most of her life, being smart meant everything to her. In fact, being smart landed her the job she had. How is being smart not good enough? Hazel thought to herself.

As if he had read her mind, Mr. Ashton said, "Everybody on my team is smart. You need to learn the system and perfect your craft. You have to know what you are doing at all times. Don't settle for figuring things out. You won't survive moments in this industry by figuring things out. You have to know that you know what you know. If you don't, you will always be a step behind and end up living a reactive life. You must know how the system works. It is time for you to intentionally be good, Hazel."

After their conversation, Hazel's boss paired her up with a work mentor and sent her back through a training program. This was humbling to Hazel, but she was willing to try it. One day, she was talking to her work mentor and became very defensive. Having her work constantly reviewed and scrutinized began to frustrate Hazel. Her work mentor noticed her frustration and pulled her to the side.

"Hazel, just trust this process. It will get you where you want to be."

Hazel looked at him and then looked away. "I just need a moment to gather my thoughts. I'm going to take an early lunch," Hazel said as she walked away.

She already knew what Byron would say, so she called her personal mentor, Darrin. Darrin had been Hazel's mentor since she was thirteen years old. In fact, Darrin was her first guidance counselor when she transferred schools. Darrin kept in contact with Hazel throughout high school and college. She always counted on his sound wisdom.

She and Darrin caught up for a few minutes then she began to explain the situation she was dealing with at work. Darrin always waited until she was done before he gave her any advice.

"Are you finished?" Darrin asked calmly.

"Yes," Hazel replied.

"Hazel, you've always been bright. I'm so extremely proud of you and all you've accomplished. The folks back home say you've made it big, but I know you've only just begun!"

They chuckled. The projects always showed Hazel major love whenever she went back to visit friends, family, or the little girls in the community.

"Hazel, we both know you've always had a tough time working on teams and getting adjusted to new environments. Unfortunately, you're not in undergrad anymore. You can't just switch classes or ask the teacher if you can work alone. This is your job, and you have bills to pay. Furthermore, this company has been around for longer than you've been alive. They know what works for their company, and you'd better figure it out if you desire to keep working for them." Darrin said.

As her mentor talked, Hazel thought quietly to herself. She was good in certain environments, but changed for the worst in environments she was not comfortable in. She knew this was true. She had dealt with this most of her life. Additionally, Hazel felt that her way of doing things was the best way. Most of her life, she had been challenged to think on her own, show initiative, and to always be assertive. She didn't know how to make the necessary shifts now.

"Hazel, think about this. What was the most thriving business chain in your hometown?" Darrin asked.

"Wilbo's, the fast food joint on the corner of fifth and ninth," Hazel replied. She loved Wilbo's as a kid. Even though it was in the middle of the projects, she and her parents always felt safe at Wilbo's. That was the one place where her father didn't mind allowing her to run and play.

"Have you been to any other Wilbo's?" Darrin asked.

"Yes, there's one close to my high school, and there were two in the same town as my college."

"Did you notice anything different between the Wilbo's in the projects and the others you've gone to?" Darrin asked.

"Of course ours in the project had extreme security, but other than that, the menus, food, beverages, uniforms, vibe, customer service, and decor were all the same," Hazel replied.

"How do you think both restaurants manage to thrive in two different areas? Is it their decor? Is it their menu or building?" Darrin asked.

"I don't know," Hazel shrugged.

"It was their system. They had different workers from different backgrounds and socioeconomic statuses, however, they all worked the same system. Methods may differ, but the mission never changes." Darrin explained.

A light bulb went off for Hazel as she remembered Wilbo's. It was the most well-kept and well-run restaurant in her old neighborhood. The same people who disrespected other establishments didn't dare get out of character at Wilbo's. It was the one place where she knew a fight wouldn't break out. Wilbo's was safe, fun, and always clean.

"How does a system survive in both environments?" Hazel asked. At this point, she realized that her mentor was really trying to help her think about her own life systems.

"The system creates an environment instead of letting its surrounding dictate how it operates. If executed well, every patron of the restaurant has the same experience regardless of their neighborhood. They are trained to work by the same standards and are given the same tools to succeed. The system addresses the universal needs and things that drive people. If anything gets off course, employees should refer back to the system and not personal feelings," Darrin explained. "When employees realize that the company is winning, they buy in even more. However, when the system begins to develop the employee, they dig in even deeper. When a company hires a rebel or someone who wants to march to their own beat, that employee sticks out like a sore thumb. Eventually, they must answer the question, "How's that working for you?" It becomes very evident that it is not. Does that make sense, Hazel?"

"Yes," she said silently. It finally all made sense to Hazel. Her conversation with Darrin was the turning point in her career. She decided to open her mind and heart and learn to be versatile.

Hazel went back to work and committed to learning the systems in place at her job. Hazel slowly started to learn how much she didn't know. The more she learned, the more her stress levels went down. Her relationships started to increase as her confidence levels began to rise. She didn't realize how many people didn't trust her work because of how defensive she was. She was no longer on edge and defensive because she wasn't afraid of not knowing an answer. She was no longer aggressive when defending how she arrived at a certain conclusion with her work. She shared her work with her team with confidence and openness to critique and questions.

Over time, she saw a significant turnaround in her career. When the time for her review came around the next year, it was a completely different situation. Not only did she get a good ranking, but she was able to use that time to provide ideas and solutions to things she thought would help the company. She had no idea, but by learning the basics of her job, buying into the culture of the company, and learning how to work their system, she capitalized on her genius. Hazel became a team player. While this was not the route she thought would get her there, trusting the process got her right where she needed to be.

LET'S TALK

Before we dig in, take a moment and answer the following questions.

- Are you living reactively instead of proactively?
- How is your stress level right now?
- Do you find yourself defensive when you are asked questions?
- Are you inwardly frustrated by the fact that you know what you need to do, know that you can do it, but you don't know how?

If you answered yes to any of the questions above, don't be alarmed. While these feelings may at times be overwhelming, it's not the end of the world for you. It's actually the beginning of your breakthrough. The beginning of a turnaround in our lives is usually marked by our ability to admit that something needs to change. We become frustrated when we try to determine how to make that change happen. Despite the frustration, you must remain consistent in your pursuit of how. Discovering how to make changes in your life is the cure for frustration, dead ends, ruts, and chaos.

Regardless of what we may convince ourselves to believe, there are systems that will work for anyone regardless of ethnicity or gender. Yes, every person experiences a different set of obstacles on their way to success. Obstacles are real things. However, we can overcome them. No matter the different obstacles we may encounter, if worked properly, the same systems will work for all of us. If something will work for anybody, it must work for everybody. Our job is not to give up. Instead, we must press through, find out how things work, and trust God to help us overcome any barrier we encounter on the way.

So, let's talk about you. You want success, right? Well, how do you plan to get it? When people tell me about their plans to become a millionaire, I always ask them, "What are you doing so well that will command a million dollars in revenue?" This question causes people to stop and think about their goals and the systems they need to incorporate to achieve them. Systems run our lives. Systems are how things work. Our dreams will be accomplished through a system. Failure or success continues to exist because of a system. Even medicine works because of a system. Everything produces its results based on a system. For instance, if you spend more than you make, you will continue to be stressed out and in debt because you are investing your money into a broken system. The key to our success is to find a system that will produce what we want, learn it, and then consistently implement it.

Dave Ramsey is a phenomenal example of what happens when you work a good system. He created a system for individuals to get out of debt. He has made a tremendous living off of Financial Peace. He developed this system by observing and analyzing the failure he'd experienced in his life. Now, he has packaged the system, and if people buy and use it, the system produces for them just as it did for him. Isn't that amazing? Though you may not realize it, right now, you are living by a system. It may be one you chose purposely, or it may be one you unconsciously adopted from your environment. For some, your system is a response to the hand life dealt you. And for others, your system is simply the result of laziness and complacency. At the end of the day, the system you live by is responsible for every aspect of your life. If you don't like what you see, it is time to change the system. Let's review the steps necessary for developing and working a system that will produce what we desire to see in our lives.

Step One: What are you currently set up to produce?

Before we can make any real changes in our lives, we must ask ourselves, "What am I currently set up to produce?" Our destiny is set, but our decisions and habits determine whether or not we will reach that destiny. Most of us know what we want, but are we set up to produce what we want? Before you dive into researching new systems, finding a life coach, and hiring a trainer, evaluate where you are now. What are the systems of your life currently producing? What results are you yielding every day?

Step Two: What's in your heart?

After you review your current level of production, make a list of what you actually want. Are you producing what you want for your life? If not, that is confirmation that something in your life needs to change. While this may appear to be the easiest step, it is actually the most difficult. As we discussed before, sometimes, we know exactly what we want, but we don't always know how it looks in our lives, or what we must do to achieve it. You must determine the end product/result you desire. This can only be done by locating what is in your heart. Your purpose in life will never change, but what is in season in your heart will change. Proverbs 13:12 (NASB) states, "Hope deferred makes the heart sick, But [a] desire fulfilled is a tree of life." Many of our hearts are sick. Sick hearts result in frustrated and stagnant lives. We end up this way because we don't know what we want or we are not set up to produce what we want.

The desires of your heart are not something man-made. The desires I am referring to come from God. It is God's way of pulling you close to Him and directing your life. Your desire is the magnetic pull to your destiny in life. Your God-given desires create a dependency on God. It is what pushes you to seek Him and develop a relationship with Him. Once you start to explore your God-given desires, He will begin to paint a vision or a picture of a preferred future for you. This preferred future becomes the roadmap for your current season. This roadmap is vital because it will guide you through every decision you make. Once you receive God's preferred future for your life, you will begin to filter every option through this vision.

Seek God and explore why you want the things you desire in this season. What is in your heart that you can't shake? John 15:16 states, "You did not choose Me, but I chose you, and appointed you that you would go and bear fruit, and that your fruit would remain, so that whatever you ask of the Father in My name He may give to you." You have been chosen by God and placed (appointed) where you are in this season of your life for a reason. You didn't ask for it. Instead, it asked for you. Discover what is in your heart and begin to prepare to bear fruit. Ask from God according to what is in your heart, and you will begin to see remarkable things happen in your life.

Step Three: Determine if you know *how* to do what is in your heart!

In our scenario, Hazel had to evaluate her life to determine if she knew how to be a team player. She finally had to admit that she didn't and had to submit to and trust a process that would set her up to be successful. You have to evaluate your current way of living and determine what you are set up to produce. As you evaluate, you must figure out what you need to learn, unlearn, or relearn to produce what you want. In order to bear the fruit mentioned in John 15, we must make sure that we have the right seed in us. We produce in life according to who we are. Who we are is based on how we see ourselves or what we believe about ourselves.

The Bible says, "As a man thinks in his heart, so is he." Therefore, it is important that you see yourself correctly. Your view of yourself, whether accurate or inaccurate, will impact what you produce in life. It is important to humble ourselves so that we can see ourselves the way God sees us in order to produce what He wants us to produce! God describes how things produce in Genesis 1:11, "Then God said, "Let the land produce vegetation: seed-bearing plants and trees on the land that bear fruit with seed in it, according to their various kinds." And it was so." Everything we see starts as a seed, and everything produces after its own kind.

Often, we assume that we possess everything we need in order to get the things we desire. Unfortunately, this is not always the case. When we have this misconception about ourselves, it causes us to be blind to the areas in which we need to grow or develop. Most of the time, we can't change it because we can't see it. This step is difficult because it causes us to turn that objective eye on ourselves.

Are you set up to bear the fruit of what's in your heart? Or, are you set up to produce the exact opposite of what you desire? Examine every intricate detail of your life. If something is not producing what you desire, get rid of it. Our friend Hazel wanted to do well on her job, and succeed in life. However, she was defensive. She was talented but not skilled. Additionally, Hazel had some credibility issues with her peers and her boss. Eventually, she had to ask herself, "How's this working for me?" It wasn't. Defending a position in life that wasn't working was getting her nowhere. She had to make some changes. She had to build her confidence by relearning some things, unlearning other things, and getting a mentor. This resulted in greater performance and confidence. Like Hazel, you have to evaluate your current behavior and belief system by your goals and make some adjustments. This is the only way you will be able to add the accountability and invest in the resources you need to improve the production of your life.

Step Four: Find or develop a system that will produce what you want.

You know what you want, you have evaluated your life, so now it is time to find a system that will produce what you want. This was easy for Hazel because there was already a system in place on her job. She just needed to trust it and commit to it. Hazel had to go back through the training program for her position, get a mentor, and have her work under constant surveillance so that she could relearn the system. The company was doing well, so the system in place worked. Hazel, however, just wasn't working the system.

The very first criteria for selecting any system is that it must be successful. Often, we make the mistake of selecting systems that have already proven to be unsuccessful. Before you adopt or commit to any system, you must check its fruit. What has that system produced for others? How have other's lives been changed because of their adoption of that particular system?

I get it. The changes you need to make may not be as hassle-free as Hazel's. After all, she was in a place that already had a system in place. I challenge you to pick one area of your life you would like to improve. Then, search for a system that works. This may require you to do research, read books, or talk to people who are successful in what you want to do. Begin to seek God for direction on where to start. Your new and improved system may come through receiving counseling, speaking with your spiritual leader, accessing a life coach, or even talking with a friend who is successful in that area. Be open to the many ways God may lead you to pinpoint the system that will work for your life.

Step Five: Work the System

In order to successfully work a system, you must discover what it takes to make systems work. Once you have located a system for your life, invest the time to learn how it works. Your job, church, athletic team, weight loss programs, etc. all have systems that create the culture for what they do. Every system, whether healthy or dysfunctional, creates a culture or environment in which things grow. The things growing may not be what you desire, but to change the product you must change the process or culture that is producing what you see. Your life is loaded with potential, and if you put it in the right culture, you will be able to achieve amazing things. In order to be developed by a culture, you must learn how things work in that culture. Every culture has a vernacular and a mindset. Anyone desiring to be a part of it must understand how it works and what it produces.

I run into individuals all the time who observe the success of others and say, "That doesn't work for people like me." If you've ever thought this way, I challenge you to dig deeper and find out what isn't working for you. In most cases, people see the results, but don't buy in and execute the process required to makes things work. Most of the time, systems don't work for us because we are just plain lazy. Laziness is probably one of the biggest reasons why certain things remain the same in our lives. We often become really excited at the beginning of trying something new, however, later on in the process, we lose the tenacity to keep working the system. Systems don't work because they are easy, they work because people work them.

Whenever you desire to make changes in your life, you will experience a level of resistance. However, you cannot allow that resistance to make you run back to your old systems. Resistance is a sign that the system is actually working. Most of the time, resistance represents a struggle between two different systems. If you are struggling to repair your credit, you may experience frustration when paying off debt, but no longer having the extra spending money you are accustomed to. If you are attempting to lose weight, you may feel resistance when you forget your healthy lunch at home and are tempted to run down the street and grab some fast food. Change the way you view the obstacles you experience on your path to transition. Adopting new systems won't be easy, but they are worth it. Systems take time to produce every portion of what you desire. You can't work a system one day and expect the world to fall into your hands. When systems are run properly over a length of time, your life will begin to respond to it. The key is not giving up and staying in the race no matter how difficult things may become.

LESSON FOUR

Do What Works

This chapter will discuss one of the most important components of making things work in your life. It is not enough to discover what is in your heart, identify what isn't working in your life, identify what does work, and learn how to work what works. You must be able to apply what works in your life.

Principle One: Learn the lesson and forget the details of the past.

I will never forget my first physics class in college, Physics 101. I knew I needed a good grade out of the class, but I didn't really apply myself. I ended up with a C. To improve my GPA, I decided to take the class over the next semester. My goal was to get an A. I had the same teacher, the class was in the same room, and it was the same material. I even sat in the same seat – I'm not kidding. I spoke with the teacher after the first class of my repeat semester, and she told me something I will never forget.

"Are your buddies from the first time you took my class going to be attending this round?" she asked.

"No ma'am," I replied.

"Good," she said. "You all laughed too much in class. If you want an A out of this class, forget everything you learned the first time."

That was the strangest thing to me. I thought I had a leg up because I had prior exposure to the information. "Why should I do that?" I asked.

"If you learned it correctly the first time, you wouldn't be back," she replied.

I took her advice and got an A the second time around. I have found this lesson to be true so many times in my life.

There is a reason we have to repeat certain seasons in our life. These repeat seasons are an opportunity for us to get things right. They are new/fresh mercy from God -- not a death sentence.

To be successful in repeats, you must approach each situation fresh. Obviously, we didn't get it right the first time. Every day we get fresh/new mercy from God. We take advantage of that fresh mercy by seeing every situation fresh. Insanity is doing the same thing the same way and expecting different results. At some point, we all have to be honest, admit when things are not working in our lives, and try something different. If what you are currently doing is not producing the desired results you want out of life, change. If it is, strengthen your resolve. We serve a God who gives fresh mercy, and you can win in every repeat situation. Make a decision to let go of distractions, lay down all your past experiences (good or bad), and see today as fresh mercy.

Principle Two: Reset your default.

Jean and her husband Bill went through an eight-week marriage life group in their church. One of the things they learned was proper communication skills. This was important because Jean had an expressive personality. People loved her, and she was full of life. Sometimes, she tended to act out of how she felt instead of what she desired. This always worked against her. Bill, on the other hand, was more quiet. He often internalized things, placed walls around his heart, and refused to let his wife all the way in his life. This hindered him from fully opening up and being himself around her.

During the life group, Jean and Bill learned how to communicate what they ultimately wanted from their spouse versus how they felt about what their spouse was or was not doing. This was crucial and life-changing. They developed a vision for their marriage and were able to develop a plan to "fight fair." They identified behaviors and words that they both agreed were out of bounds. They agreed that the "out of bounds" words and behaviors wouldn't allow them to accomplish their vision for their marriage. Whenever either of them saw themselves "out of bounds," there was no debate about who was in the wrong. They told their close friends about the agreement to add an added measure of accountability. After the session, things were going great! They were talking, enjoying each other, staying "in bounds," and growing together seemingly until an event with friends just one week after their life group ended.

Jean looked across the room and noticed Bill, the introvert, being the life of the party. He was laughing, telling jokes, and having the time of his life. For some reason, this infuriated Jean. The more he laughed, the worse her night got. In her eyes, Bill never laughed like that with her. He was never that relaxed. "How could the man I plan to spend the rest of my life with be so relaxed with everyone but me?" she asked herself. Finally, she couldn't take it anymore. She went and joined the group Bill was a part of to see if Bill would pull back into his shell. Just as she predicted, he stopped making jokes and went back to being the Bill she knew. Well, this pushed Jean over the top. She looked at Bill and said, "I am ready to go!"

"No, I am not ready," Bill replied.

So, Jean left the group and sat with her friends. One of her good friends, Estelle asked, "What's wrong with you, Jean?"

Jean broke down and explained the situation. Estelle seemed unmoved by Jean's emotion. As one of their sources of accountability, she was privy to their vision and fighting fair agreement. She looked at Jean's and said, "In light of your vision and fighting fair agreement, how's this attitude working for you?"

Jean had to laugh because she knew it wasn't. As a matter of fact, it was getting her the exact opposite of what she wanted.

"If you want him to relax around you, find out why he shuts down around you. Don't follow your feelings. Follow your desire and use what you learned in your life group," Estelle said.

That hit Jean like a ton of bricks. In her moment of frustration, she totally disregarded everything she had learned and went with her current emotion. She followed Estelle's advice, used what she learned in the life group, and got Bill to finally let his guard down around her. Of course, this didn't happen in one conversation, but over time, Bill really began to open up around her. She had to remind herself of this every time she got frustrated, and Bill was also able to do the same thing when he was tempted to shut down.

This scenario happens to people every day! In times of pressure and testing, we have to remember to go with what works and not how we feel. What you feel is not always what is right. Every feeling you have is real. However just because it is real doesn't make it right. You want to do what is right at times over what is real. Your feelings will change, so they should not be your guide. Your prior system for dealing with issues can be a comfort zone that causes you to forget the new systems you've learned. Be sure to keep a fresh set of eyes on your life. Everybody needs an Estelle! You need someone who has an objective view of things to help you keep your focus because we tend to be further along in our heads than we are in our reality!

Principle Three: Trust the process.

I had the opportunity to speak to an extraordinary athlete his senior year of college. "Now that you are a senior, if you had the opportunity, what would you go back and tell your freshman self?"

"Trust the process," he replied. "The process works if you let it. There were days when I felt like quitting. There were times when I felt like my coach didn't like me, everyone was against me, and that none of this (early morning workouts, extra practices, tutoring, school, etc.) was worth it. However, now I see it pay off. It was all worth it."

I want to encourage you to do the same thing. Trust the process. The coaches in this athlete's life had designed a process to produce a team culture and environment that would produce championships, people of character, and great team chemistry. Every process that works has an end result. You are surrounded by process. If you go to a trainer and they put you on a workout regimen, you stick to that regimen. Why? Because you know they have developed a program that will produce the result you are looking for.

Trusting the process is adhering to the plan. Desiring better is not a guarantee that better will show up. You have to find a process that will produce better and trust it enough to stick to it until you see the results -- even when it makes you uncomfortable.

Often, it takes many so long to trust the process. For this reason, most people don't identify what does work until after failure occurs. We can either change by crisis or by wisdom. Unfortunately, most change by crisis. It isn't until the pain of remaining the same becomes greater than the pain of change that most people change.

What you are going through is not pointless, but you have to know where the process is trying to take you. Also, how you go through is just as important as what you go through. Trust me, it is going to be worth it in the end. Stay the course, do what works, and watch what you are working begin to work for you.

The Deception of Potential

In my life, I have had to learn many things the hard way. I have had some retrospect "How's that working for you?" moments that make me cringe. Like most people, I have always been pretty aware of my potential. I spend a lot of time dreaming. My dreams are vivid and are an active part of my life. However, dreaming can be deceptive if you don't have a grind to match the level of your dream. Dreaming builds your confidence because it exposes your potential. It shows you what could be. The only challenge is you still have to deal with what is. Therein lies the challenge for so many of us. How do we get from the "what is" to the "can be"?

If we are not careful, we will end up living life drunk off potential and never sober up to make potential a reality. Potential is intoxicating because we can deceive ourselves into thinking we are further along in life than we really are. This can lead to frustration with people if they don't respond to us correctly. Apparently, they don't see what we see and don't seem to respect our vision and dreams. Here's an important fact to know: People cannot see what you see regarding yourself. The only thing they know is what you tell them. People will only follow if you can prove your ability to make your dreams a reality.

In many cases, our dreams are drowned by the inadequacies of our current reality. As a result, we have no credibility because our production doesn't match our potential. This lack of credibility doesn't stop the flow of ideas, potential, and power in our lives, it just clogs the flow of our desires being fulfilled.

Stop right now and ask yourself: Does my production equal my potential? By not asking myself this question, I have fallen into the trap of arrogance. This is a horrible place to be. Arrogance causes us to stop growing. We don't realize it because we shut out wise counsel and write constructive criticism off as people hating or not "understanding" our path in life. We are left to learn from our experiences which, in most cases, ends in failure.

Honestly, there are many failures I could have avoided in life if I was aware of my immaturity. I have discovered that it is possible to have mature dreams and live an immature life. Many of the convictions I once had were based on immaturity. I wish I would have let people challenge me so that I could fully develop and see life from different perspectives. I became judgmental and critical of people and came off as a know it all. I had to suffer the shame of a lot of my ideas failing and dreams turning into nightmares.

I have the luxury of talking to people daily, and it is so hard to get through to many because they are sold on their dreams, as they should be. However, they are blinded to their reality. Sometimes I want to scream, "I know where you are!" Our dreams make us feel special, and we are all special, but we all succeed or fail based on the same principles.

What many people call faith is foolishness on steroids. Faith starts with a dream, but it is always followed by a plan. If you don't have a plan and a proper assessment of yourself along with your dreams, you will live in frustration and always have an excuse for why things aren't happening. You can be coached through mistakes, but no one can help you with your excuses. Excuses put the responsibility for change on whatever or whomever you are blaming and leaves you powerless. Many people don't realize when they are in this state. I want to give you a few things to consider if you fall into this category.

- Do you see less talented people getting selected for things you know you could do better than them?
- Do you find yourself being defensive when people question your work or word?
- Have you ever stopped to analyze the feedback you consistently get from people, even your haters?
- Can you separate your work from who you are as a person?
- Are you seeing your influence and responsibility diminishing and you blame it on people being jealous of you or not being able to handle you?
- Do you find yourself telling people "they don't know my worth" or "they don't know what they are sleeping on within this organization?"

After you ask yourself these questions take an honest evaluation of your life and see if you are doing any of the following things at home, work, church, or any part of your life.

- Am I pulling away because people don't seem to get me? Take a look at the last tasks you have been asked to complete and ask yourself, "Did I put out quality work? Did I even do what was asked of me? Did I just give them what I thought they needed instead of what they asked for?"
- Is my quality of work riding the wave of my emotions? I went into a coffee shop one day and ordered a hot chocolate. The lady that waited on

me had a look on her face that let everyone know that she was having a bad day. I got my hot chocolate and got in my car. When I got down the road, I tasted it and it was by far the worst hot chocolate ever. I knew something was wrong because of the look on her face when she gave it to me. The same thing happens when your emotions get in the way of your performance.

- Have you ever said, "If I weren't here, this place would fall apart!"? Although this statement could be true, it is also a reflection of your leadership. You could be carrying too much, and that could be part of your stress in your situation. Nothing we do should be hinged on one person. You should always have a system in place that produces what needs to be done, and people run that system -- not one person. A system is a method of principles and procedures that produce quality work every time. For instance, Longhorn has a system that produces the same tasting parmesan crusted chicken in Tennessee as it does in Alabama. If the cook quits or gets mad, someone else can come in with cooking skills and follow the system to produce the same parmesan crusted chicken. Quality doesn't suffer. You need a system in place that produces order.

- Can we be honest? You may also be dealing with control issues or a need to prove yourself that isn't allowing you to include others in what you are dealing with! We all have issues that contribute to our situations. It may not be the cause of the situation you are in, but your issues help fan the flames. Yes, your situation may be toxic, but you don't have to be toxic. The favor of God will cause you to rise in any situation.

- Am I starting to generalize all things? (relationships, churches, companies). When you experience failure, rejection, or hurt, it is easy to lump things of the same kind together. The reality is, you may keep having the same experience in a particular area, but remember you are the one picking these experiences. Perhaps you keep picking more of the same kind and need to learn wisdom on how to make decisions.

- Do I come into situations telling people what needs to be done? Or, am I sitting back and observing how things are done? If you don't take the time to get to know the culture of wherever you are, you will be shut out of opportunities -- and not because people don't respect your gift or want your ideas. It may be because you will take things in a direction different than they want to go or they may even be doing what you are suggesting differently than you are accustomed to. If you don't figure out the culture, you may exit places prematurely and leave thinking that they didn't accept you and your ideas. Your assessment could be so far from the truth! You have to learn how to adjust to the culture without changing who you are.

Your life can work as well as your dreams and potential work. You just have to learn how to work it by being honest with yourself about where you are. Refuse to make excuses when you know there is more to you than what you are currently releasing.

CLOSING

Over the course of this book, I pray something clicked for you. I desire that we will all become self-aware so we can reach our God-given destiny. Unfortunately, many people are experts at others' lives and novices at living their own. We can easily see what to fix in others' lives and miss glaring deficiencies in our own. I hope that through the stories and lessons presented, you saw yourself and learned principles that can help change your life. I wanted this book to feel like you and I were having a conversation. Obviously, we can't hear each other, but I hoped reading this book would feel like you and I were sitting across from each other discussing an area of your life that you feel stuck in or want to see progress! I believe that after reading this book, in every situation in life where you are seeking progress and success, you will be able to figure out what you want as an outcome and then ask yourself these four questions:

- What does not work or what am I doing that is not working?
- What does work and will produce what I desire?
- Do I know how to work what works?
- Am I doing what works?

If you can build this system into your subconscious, you will find great success in life and avoid cycles that waste a lot of your time, energy, and resources. Don't let the word subconscious run you off. Your subconscious is where you store information that you use without even thinking about it on a daily basis. For instance, at a traffic light because you have accepted the traffic rules as true, your mind knows red means stop, yellow means speed up (just kidding) slow down, and green means go. If you will be honest with yourself and swallow your pride in every situation, using this system should help you reach your full potential and accomplish your God-given desires.

ABOUT THE AUTHOR

Jason D. Scales is a native of Shelbyville, TN. He currently resides in Murfreesboro, TN. He is the husband of Barbara A. Scales and the proud father of Isaiah Scales. Jason pastors the Believers Faith Fellowship Church in Christiana, TN. He earned a B.S. in Psychology and MBA at the University of Tennessee at Chattanooga.

Pastor Scales has a heart to teach people with simplicity and power. His desire is for everyone to have an intimate relationship with Jesus Christ, be passionate in their worship, sincere in their praise, wise in their decision making, and purposeful in their living. This is his second book. His first published work, Resilient: How to Bounce Back from Loss, is available for purchase on Amazon. To learn more about Jason and his book visit www.jdscales.com/howbook.

STAY CONNECTED

Thank you for purchasing, *How's That Working for You?* Jason would like to connect with you! Below are a few ways you can connect with Jason, stay updated on new releases, and get information on upcoming events!

FACEBOOK Jason Scales

INSTAGRAM @jscales3

EMAIL jscales3@yahoo.com

WEBSITE www.jdscales.com/howbook

www.bfftn.org